Fun Felt Crafts:

Penny Rugs and Pretty Things from Recycled Wool

D1224399

Fun Felt Crafts:
Penny Rugs and Pretty Things from Recycled Wool

Tina Skinner

4880 Lower Valley Road · Atglen, PA · 19310

I would like to thank my talented models, Courtney Rowland, Tricia Oswald, and Holly Dastalfo, who made my projects look so beautiful.

Schiffer Books are available at special discounts for bulk purchases for sales promotions or premiums. Special editions, including personalized covers, corporate imprints, and excerpts can be created in large quantities for special needs. For more information contact the publisher:

Published by Schiffer Publishing Ltd.
4880 Lower Valley Road
Atglen, PA 19310
Phone: (610) 593-1777; Fax: (610) 593-2002
E-mail: Info@schifferbooks.com

For the largest selection of fine reference books on this and related subjects, please visit our web site at **www.schifferbooks.com**
We are always looking for people to write books on new and related subjects. If you have an idea for a book please contact us at the above address.

This book may be purchased from the publisher.
Include $5.00 for shipping.
Please try your bookstore first.
You may write for a free catalog.

In Europe, Schiffer books are distributed by
Bushwood Books
6 Marksbury Ave.
Kew Gardens
Surrey TW9 4JF England
Phone: 44 (0) 20 8392 8585; Fax: 44 (0) 20 8392 9876
E-mail: info@bushwoodbooks.co.uk
Website: www.bushwoodbooks.co.uk

Designed by RoS
Type set in BenguiatGot Bk BT/Humanist 521 BT

ISBN: 978-0-7643-3299-9
Printed in China

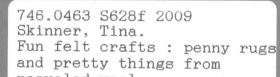

Contents

An ambitious project, this was one of Janice Sonnen's first penny rugs. She cut out over 615 circles, with scissors of course, and carefully stitched them into a penny rug approximately 40 inches long. It is backed in cotton, and one must touch and hold to truly appreciate the luxury of these lovingly rich rings of wool.

Introduction

A History of Wool Craft

Felt is one of the most popular craft mediums right now, but it's hardly a flash-in-the-pan trend. Sheep are one of mankind's oldest commodities, and their wonderful wool has been clothing and sheltering us throughout recorded history. Saving scraps of wool from sewing projects and salvaging what's usable from used-up clothes is an age-old tradition. Women have been recycling wool into clever crafts since time immemorial, and the styles pioneered by America's early homemakers are still much admired and imitated in crafting circles today. Besides forming the basis for hooked and braided rugs, wool scraps are also the stars of the lesser-known penny rug. Penny rugs were probably never destined for work on the floor. Rather, they were used to protect the tops of precious cabinetry or furnishings while showing off the mistress's skill with a needle.

Janice E. Sonnen, a juried craftsman whose work follows the time-honored traditions and aesthetics of American Primitive style, graciously allowed me to include some of her work to help illustrate original penny rug artistry. Early Americans would use coins as templates for various-sized circles cut out of wool, then stack and stitch these circles. The concentric rings still echo in the most contemporary of art, and still charm in their original palettes of vegetal tones. In addition to the coin shape, penny rugs often were weighted with pennies between their layers to improve the way they lay across the back of a chair or across a table top. Janice still inserts a penny in every piece she makes, inviting those who admire her work at craft shows to guess where it's hidden. You can see more of her work at sonnen.rbcrafts.org.

The wools I have salvaged from thrift shops and my own castoffs have called me in more contemporary directions. With two young daughters, there's plenty of pink in my palette. I've also enjoyed developing smaller projects that are easy to give as gifts, and that seem to sell easily on consignment in local gift shops.

I find it eminently satisfying to sit, needle in hand, and work with wool. The textile has a wonderful texture, and a row of even stitches gives me a fleeting moment of pride. I tell people I haven't watched TV in ages, but I listen to it almost every night as I work on my creations. I find it hard to rest easy if I haven't made something before I go to bed. It's also hard to sleep when, after making something new, I'm excited by ideas for the next project.

I hope that the basic skills outlined in this book fire you up with a similar passion to play and create with felt. Your own tastes will guide your hand as you seek out wool garments that are ready for reuse. You may find yourself intrigued by dyeing, or by needle felting. Like me, you'll probably want to try it all. Find your local fiber guild and join in with other women passionate about working with textiles. There you'll find women like Janice and myself who'll show you new directions to try as you branch out to create your own crafts. Welcome to our multi-generational guild, and enjoy the journey.

Although animals are not her favorite subjects to portray, artist Janice Sonnen has done a wonderful job of capturing the primitive style typical of early American craft. Sheep and tulip trees are common motifs.

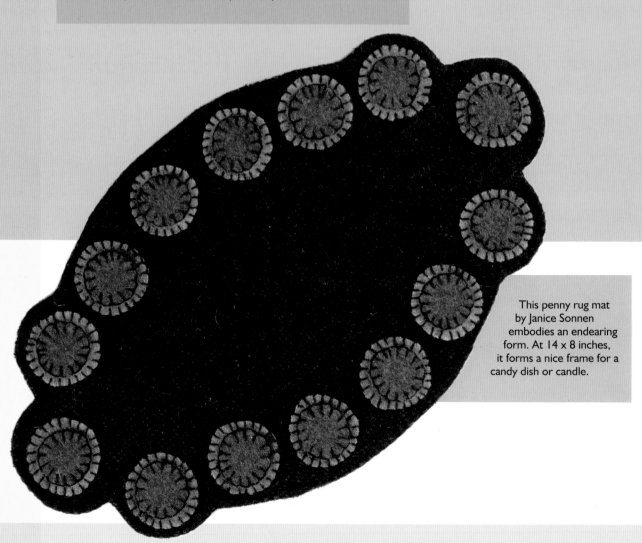

This penny rug mat by Janice Sonnen embodies an endearing form. At 14 x 8 inches, it forms a nice frame for a candy dish or candle.

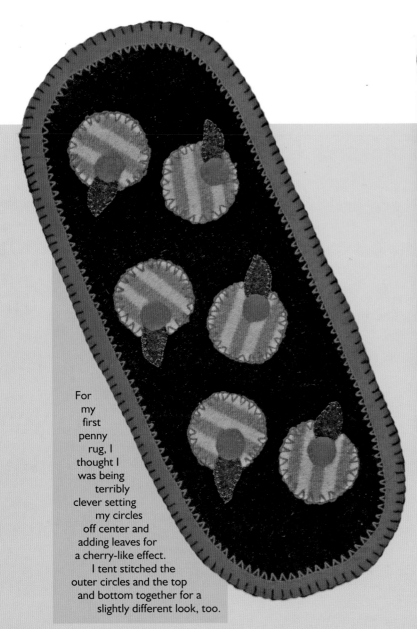

For my first penny rug, I thought I was being terribly clever setting my circles off center and adding leaves for a cherry-like effect. I tent stitched the outer circles and the top and bottom together for a slightly different look, too.

I liked the peppermint candy colors of this green, red, and white combination. My gingerbread folk, fashioned from men's suiting, look as though they overindulged in sugar.

Squirrels are a favorite of my mother-in-law, who also appreciates primitive style. I created this table runner for her Christmas buffet, using antique squirrel art for inspiration.

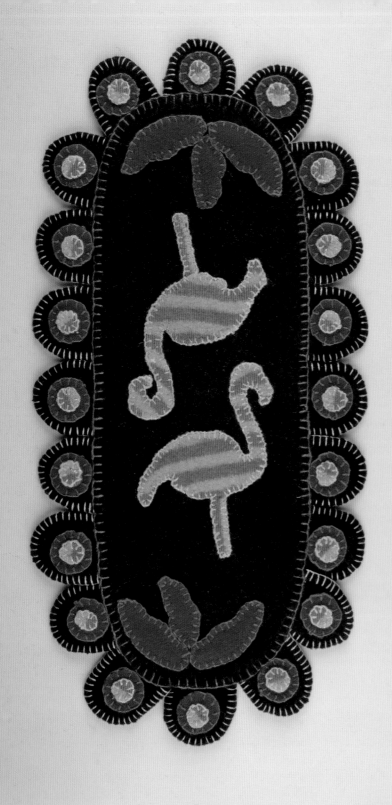

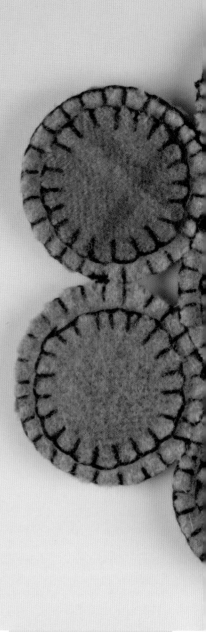

Pennies are stitched together into a candle mat by Janice Sonnen.

This penny rug took many, many hours. I created each tongue separately and joined them to the rug when I added backing. The flamingoes and tropical palm shapes created a fun challenge. Using metallic thread created a wonderful, shimmery, tacky effect, but metallic thread is more challenging than nice, grippy yarn. Wait to try this one until after you've completed a few other projects.

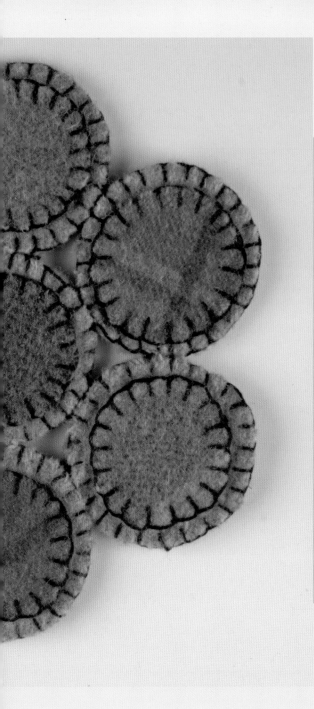

The tongues that protrude from either end of this placemat by Janice Sonnen are another repeating motif found in primitive textiles.

Before, a nice wool jacket assembled in Poland.

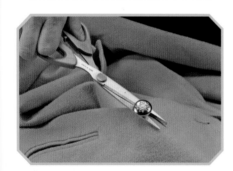

After, a disassembled jacket that has been washed and folded. In front are a sleeve panel and a small piece salvaged from the collar.

In a less formal society, wool jackets and blazers are a dime a dozen. Well, almost. This one cost 75 cents at a Goodwill. This wool was felted before the jacket was made, but a good washing will felt it more, making it thicker, sturdier, and ready for many versatile projects.

Remove the buttons first. These are great keepers. Often a jacket's buttons can be reused with the same wool later, for an accent button, or the closure on a pouch or clasp. Try to cut it off without damaging the wool.

Starting at the bottom hem, rip out the satin lining. Sometimes you need to use scissors if a reinforced corner starts to rip into the wool. I'm usually able to remove the entire lining in under a minute without using the scissors at all.

By turning the sleeves inside out, I am able to pull the lining apart. I find this is easiest by dropping the jacket to the floor, stepping on the sleeves, and yanking the lining free.

Recycling Wool

The other night I was working with a red yarn from a brand new skein. The paper band had a price tag on it, $1.29, and the price tag named the seller – Jamesway. Eager crafters tend to buy more yarn than they can ever hope to knit or crochet. We all have stashes of lush, soft, shiny, stuff that intrigued us, though we never had time to put it to use. Yarn leftovers, and even brand-new skeins, are easy to find at yard sales and in thrift shops. Grab bargains and stock up on some colors that appeal to you. It's nice to pick through shelves and drawers, mixing and matching fabrics, threads, and accessories. You don't need a lot to get started, but once you do you'll probably always have too much.

Likewise, wool fabrics are often cast aside. A size 14 women's wool skirt is a virtual treasure. Whites and creams are to-die-for, if you are into dying. Big wool coats, perhaps shabby with wear, make wonderful, thick wool to cut up and play with. Read the labels. You want a minimum of 90 percent wool to get a good felt, though blends that include angora (rabbit), cashmere (goat), and alpaca fibers felt nicely, too, and create thick, soft fabrics that are dreamy to work with. Sweaters, even when they are shrunk up and thickened by felting, still have a great stretchy quality, and they offer ribbed necks, cuffs, and waistlines that are really fun to play with.

Although I've thrown lots of other finished projects in to inspire you, most of the projects in this book were created from just a few recycled garments. There's lots left over, too. Depending on the size of your pieces, one garment goes a really, really long way.

Wool is an incredibly durable, natural, renewable resource. It takes forever to decompose – think about the hair they find on ancient mummies! And the fibers are incredibly strong. However, it has one enemy: moths. Protect your investment by storing it in a dry area with some aromatic herbs like cinnamon and lavender to throw those pests off track. And never introduce recently acquired wool to your stash without washing it first – it might be carrying the eggs of these winged wool-munchers.

Wash your wool in hot, hot water. The hot water, a little detergent, and the agitation of the washing machine are what bind the barbed fibers of wool, condensing the fabric. If you've ever accidentally washed a wool sweater and brought out a garment too small for your child, you know how well it can work.

  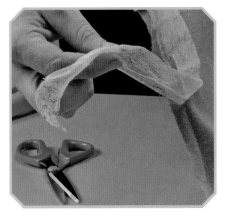

You'll quickly come to appreciate the effort and time that goes into making a jacket, while you take only a few minutes to utterly destroy it! This is a wonderful jacket for recycled wool. The back panel has no darts and is all one piece.

Cut into the seams to begin a separation, and the rest of the seam will simply rip open. You'll feel the difference between cutting wool versus the more desirable cutting of the threads that bind the pieces. Take apart all the pieces of the jacket this way. It's your call whether you want to fuss over the small pieces that can be gleaned from collars and pocket tabs. If I find the interfacing difficult, I'm likely to scrap them. If the color is inspiring, I glean every small piece.

Now is the time to remove as much interfacing as you can before washing. Some are particularly difficult, while others come away easily. Your fabric will shrink more evenly and won't require as much ironing if you get the facing out now. If it's too challenging, you can always try washing it and see if the result can be salvaged afterward. Some pull away easily while the fabric is still wet after washing. For the most difficult interfacings, I simply leave them on, iron the fabric, and use the felt in projects where the back won't show.

Before: skirts offer nice wool panels. This is a small skirt. The kick pleat cuts down on the suability of the fabric, but since it's such a wonderful red, I couldn't resist. You can never get too much red for flowers, Christmas projects, Valentines Day, etc....

After: The color bled considerably during the wash process. The results are always unpredictable, and thus fun!

Before: A foot-long ruler measures a child's sweater before washing. I usually disassemble a sweater for washing, but I left this one intact to illustrate the shrinkage. It varies every time, based on the tightness of the knit and the quality of the wool.

After: the sweater has shrunk considerably more in the bodice than the sleeves, which remain long.

Before: a wonderful, big sweater is turned inside out to prepare for felting. The shoulder pads are removed easily using scissors. The sweater is cut up along the seams. I cut beside sweater seams – after the seams felt they make interesting rope-like elements for projects. Even the seam running the length of the sleeve has been opened.

This one shrank by at least half because the knit was so loose. There is considerable fraying along the cut edges, but the sweater has felted up into a nice, thick textile.

Basic Stitches

It will only take you an hour or so to become a master of the basic stitches you need to create the projects in this book. As you proceed with a row of blanket stitches, look back over your work every 5 or 6 stitches. If a stitch is too short or too long, go back and fix it. It's easy to pull stitches out, and you'll be happier with the finished product. Plus, the punishment of redoing your work is going to make you better going forward.

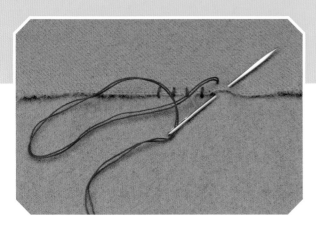

Whip stitch

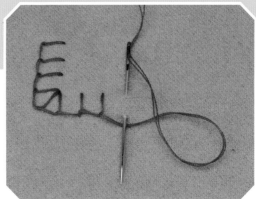

Basic blanket stitch

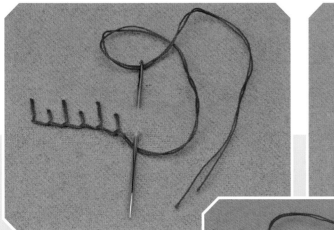

Varied blanket stitch

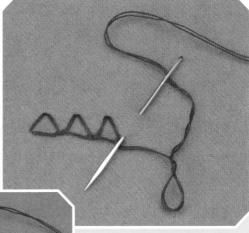

Tent blanket stitch

Feather stitch

Starting with Circles

Simple Christmas ornaments are great ways to practice your stitching. Small, circular ornaments mimic the original "pennies" women fashioned for showy parlor textiles centuries ago, and contribute to a sense of instant success. Have fun playing with felt, yarns, buttons, and beads. There's lots of room to be creative while you work on perfecting the spacing and evenness of your blanket-stitching skills. After salvaging a nice green wool coat and a woolen, red men's work shirt, I made dozens of ornaments and still have a wealth of leftovers for future projects. When you're done, you'll have a pile of great holiday gifts to give. These little treasures also serve as a great substitute for a store-bought bow on a package. You can also attach one to a Christmas card and send a personal keepsake.

Trace two circles onto freezer paper, iron on felt and then cut out. I used a saltshaker and a spice lid to create these two complementary sizes. Then choose a contrasting button to match. You will need two larger circles for front and back, and one or two of the smaller circles depending on whether you want to embellish the back.

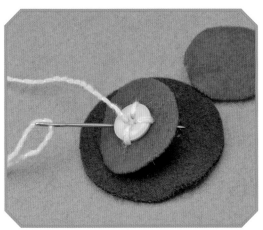

Sew the button on first. Because this button will never have to go through a buttonhole, you can sew it on in a more decorative way.

Cool Tip

You can always pin your pattern to the fabric to cut it out. However, to make things really easy, and to get more perfect cuts, invest in a three-dollar roll of freezer paper, available in most grocery stores. Waxed on one side, the paper is transparent enough that you can trace your pattern onto the dull side, attach the design to your felt with a warm iron, and then cut out. You can even reuse the patterns time and time again.

After creating lots of off-center circles, I finally realized the importance of pinning the center circle to the outer one to keep it from migrating during the initial stitching.

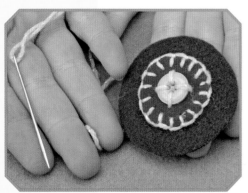

Blanket stitch inner circle to outer.

If you like, embellish the central circle with another row of blanket stitching, if you want a two-sided ornament do the same to the back circle, then attach the front to the back circle with a final round of stitches.

Here are some of many possible variations on the circular ornament. Small beads dot little Christmas trees, metallic threads add shimmer, and triple circles add depth. The yin-yang design was challenging – the point of the overlay requires a small, hidden stitch to anchor it in place.

After knotting the last blanket stitch to the first, feed the remaining string between the layers and through the center of the bottom disk and trim, or use it to create a hanger. In this case, I did not have enough to create a loop for hanging on the Christmas tree, so I clipped it off.

Add a loop for hanging and the ornament is done.

Leaf shapes are wonderful tree ornaments, but can also be used as brooches, table ornaments, or embellishments on hats or scarves. Have fun – these wooly creations evoke a strong appeal throughout fall and winter. I created my patterns by picking up a few attractive leaves in my own yard and then tracing them with simplified lines that made it easier to stitch them. Two pieces of felt are cut out back to back. Before blanket-stitching the edges, try featherstitch veins in a decorative thread.

Graduation Projects

When you're ready to start challenging yourself, start working on more complicated Christmas shapes. Following are a couple of fun projects I enjoyed. The holidays offer endless inspiration. Break out your cookie cutter collection and you've got templates for wonderful seasonal ornaments. Trace them onto paper, or directly to your fabric, and get stitching.

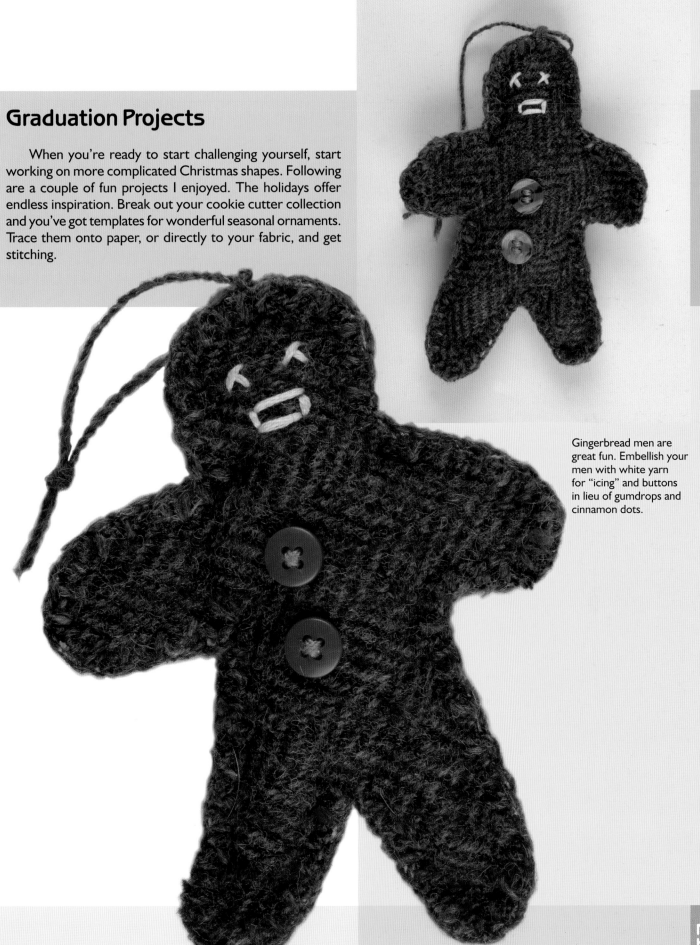

Gingerbread men are great fun. Embellish your men with white yarn for "icing" and buttons in lieu of gumdrops and cinnamon dots.

After you've mastered the circle, you can start branching out. A heart is the next logical step in skill development. Stacked hearts are endearing, they make great gifts for Valentines and any other time of the year when you want to express love. Trace the patterns included, or simply fold and cut your own hearts.

We'll use three pieces of the felt we made in the first chapter to make a heart. A nice thick piece will form the largest piece to give the brooch stability.

Pattern Template 1

Simple Three-Tiered Heart

You can work with freezer paper, or simply fold the fabric and fashion your first, inner-circle heart as shown. Folding the fabric makes the heart symmetrical, and the shape can be refolded and trimmed until you have a heart that pleases you.

Using your first heart as a guideline, pinch next to a folded piece of your second fabric and cut out a larger heart.

Open the pieces and fit them together, trimming until you are pleased with the match.

Using the same method, cut and trim the third piece in the trio, using the second, central piece as a guide.

Trim until the pieces are roughly as you like them. Don't trim too closely as the hearts may shift when you are sewing and you'll want to adjust by trimming more later.

Sew your pin back on first. Secure the first heart to the second with two pins to keep it from shifting.

Blanket stitch around the heart. Secure the point at the bottom of the heart in place with an extra loop to make sure that it doesn't shift. Trim the second heart, if you need to, for a pleasing symmetry.

Secure the second heart to the third and proceed to blanket stitch around it.

Create a nice finished look in back by threading your string several times through the stitches on the third heart.

After several passes through the back loops, secure and trim the remaining thread.

Finally, blanket stitch around the third heart. Because this piece of wool is so thick, I am able to feed my remaining thread through the actual fabric and up through the center to trim off the tail. I use small scissors to trim away excess felt between the stitches – carefully – to give it a finished look.

Finished!

Working with Ribbon

Ribbons and hearts are a wonderful marriage, with the sheen of the ribbon creating a great contrast with the more textural, soft wool. Thin satin ribbon is available in craft and sewing stores, and you'll have lots of fun playing with it. A little care needs to be taken during each loop of the blanket stitch to make sure the ribbon is twisted in a way that pleases you, but you'll quickly create loveable projects.

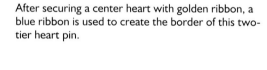

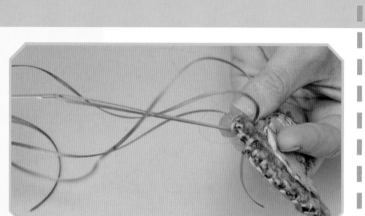

After securing a center heart with golden ribbon, a blue ribbon is used to create the border of this two-tier heart pin.

The ribbon is secured with a double knot between first and last stitches.

Trimmed ends of the ribbon are hidden by passing under stitches and through the thick wool before cutting.

Fringe on a Heart

A wonderful border for your heart can be crafted using the ribbed edges of sweaters. In this case, the collar of the children's sweater we shrunk is easily separated and scored to give a dramatic outline to our heart. Also, a stripe from that sweater gives us a fun, red-and-white center heart for our three-tiered creation.

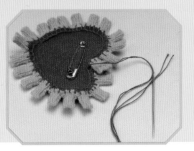

After securing the fringe, I finish the back and add stability to the piece by running extra thread under the stitches.

The knit trim on the children's sweater collar is trimmed closely and paired with matching felt hearts.

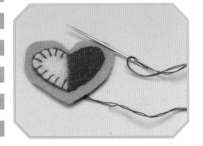

The top two hearts are sewn together.

For the first step, secure the pin back to the base heart.

Secure the top two hearts to the base with pins before blanket stitching.

Slots are cut in the collar, carefully centered between the ribs and to a quarter inch from the base.

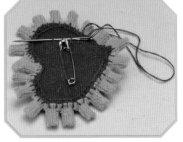

After stitching the front, give the back a finish look by looping through the base stitches several times around before trimming off the remaining thread.

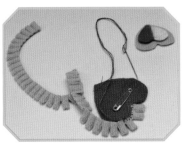

These stitches will show, so it's important that your blanket stitches be fairly uniform. Work with your piece lying on a flat surface to help create perfect alignment and a piece that will lie flat. The fringe could be positioned with either side facing out. I chose the hollowed out side for the front because it seemed more dramatic

You may be the only one who ever looks at it, but this is a nice back, celebrating your time and attention, and the handmade nature of this adornment.

Making a Pouch

A handy little pouch is easy to create, and you'll never run out of uses for it. I love organizing my necklaces in pouches to keep them from tangling. There's always stuff that needs organizing in the purse, too. A pouch is a wonderful way to give a small gift to someone, too. This pouch gets a little body by doubling the fabric and inserting a piece of recycled plastic, and a little bling from metallic thread and the button from the jacket that produced this recycled wool.

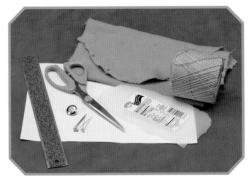

What you'll need: A straight-edge ruler and standard piece of 8 1/2" x 11" paper (recycle something!), a piece of flat plastic cut from a cider carton, pins and needle, decorative thread, wool panels (enough for a doubled project), and good sharp scissors.

Make your own pattern by first determining how wide you want your purse to be, then use the straight edge of the ruler to rip away the remainder of the paper.

Fold the bottom third or more up to determine the depth of your purse, then fold in the corners of what will become the purse clasp.

Cut your plastic to fit within the back panel of the purse. You should have an allowance of at least half an inch on all sides.

Pin your pattern to a double layer of fabric and cut it out.

Fold your purse to its final size and pin the front and back together. Now is a good time to trim the purse flap to a shape you find desirable. I like the corners rounded; they are easier to sew.

Insert the plastic piece between the two pieces of the back panel and pin in place.

Sew the button into position on the outside piece of fabric for the pouch flap. Tie in place and cut off the excess thread.

Begin sewing the pouch by feeding your string through one layer of fabric to hide the end. Let the remainder of the string stick out until you are done sewing – it helps you to control the tension and ensure that your first stitch won't slip out.

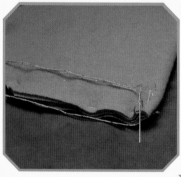

Your first stitch is a small knot. The string is fed through all four layers and then looped back through itself to secure it. Stay close to the corner.

Use your fingers to hold the first stitch taunt and straight while you make the next one.

Continue to sew up the side, around the flap, and down the other side.

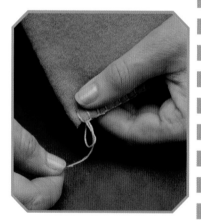

Finish at the bottom corner with another looped knot.

Feed excess string back between layers of cloth and cut level with fabric.

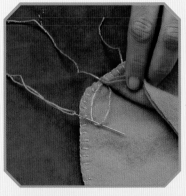

To sew the top opening of the pouch, feed the string up under the stitches and knot to the uppermost stitch along the side, hiding the knot inside the purse.

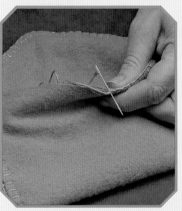

Because I used too short a piece of string, I need to tie it off halfway. Create a knot at the end of the last stitch and hide the end between the layers.

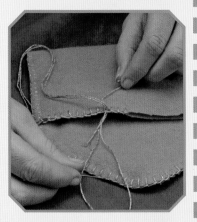

Knot the new string to an earlier stitch and feed the thread between the layers of fabric.

The new piece of string comes up behind the new stitch, ready to continue the blanket stitching.

Finish the end with a knot on a side stitch and hide the excess string as before.

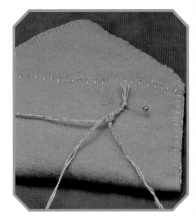

Six strands of matching thread are knotted together and pinned down to enable braiding.

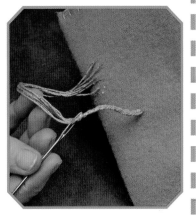

A large needle is used to accommodate the braid. After carefully measuring where the bottom of the clasp falls, feed the braid through just off center and pull until the knot is snug against the inside fabric.

Feed the braid back through and knot on the inside after measuring that the loop will fit comfortably over the button. The loop base should not be as wide as the button to prevent slippage. Cut off excess string inside the purse.

Men's suits get up-cycled with contrasting threads and matching buttons.

Bright, fluffy sweater felt is trimmed in rainbow-colored silk ribbon for colorful, fun purses.

A more formal clasp pairs a striped sweater with red coat wool. Prominent black stitches fall short of perfect in order to highlight the item's handmade nature. If you want to hide your stitches, use matching threads.

Flower Power

Flowers are my very favorite thing to make. The widths and characters of the many felts in my stash, the selection of colored string, and several basic techniques means that I can create something entirely new every time I sit down with a new project. The following projects illustrate ways to work with a variety of bases and petals styles. Try mastering these techniques, and then let your own imagination and the materials at hand take over.

The flowers shown in this vignette were all created using loops cut from the ribbed cuffs and waistlines of sweaters.

Loopy Blooms

Working off a simple stem and leaf base, we'll coil doubled strands of scored wool into a circle and, voila, adorable. One of the easiest things to use is the ribbed cuff or waistline of a sweater to create the scored petals, though these two projects shown use straight cut lengths of felt. We're making the piece on the left using the gold jacket we cut up to form the petals and the white yarn. The flower on the right was made with strips from an angora sweater and was stitched using a more subtle green and white embroidery floss. Both have

Pattern Template 3

bases from the same wonderful, green angora dress that shrunk up thick and beautiful.

Trace the pattern for the stem and leaf base onto freezer paper and iron to your felt. This green angora fabric is the soft, lush result of a drastically shrunken dress.

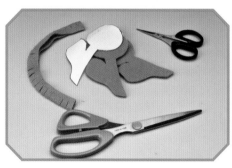

In addition to two bases, cut two petal strips 1 1/2" wide by about 10" long, or one 16" strip. Then score them with small scissors to create petals.

Attach pin back to one piece of the base. Attach the first layer of petals to the other. Keep your stitches small so they won't show behind the second layer of petals. Cut the last petal to sit flush with the first and stitch carefully into place.

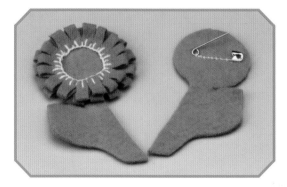

Try varying your stitches for the second layer of petals – make a longer stitch for the center of the petal and a shorter stitch in between.

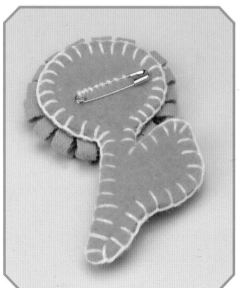

Blanket stitch the two base pieces together.

Petals in a Row

In this technique, a ribbon of single layer petals is coiled on a base to create a multi-dimensional flower. The white flower above has a string of petals carefully folded in a circle on a yellow base. The edges of this fluffy sweater fabric were covered in the center with a big, shiny button.

A rainbow sweater yields a colorful rainbow brooch.

Start out with red thread, the striped sweater, the pocket from the red skirt, and a pin back.

Cutting next to the shoulder seam, remove a sleeve from the sweater, then cut down the sweater seam to open the sleeve up.

After opening up the sleeve along the seam, cut a strip approximately 1 1/4 inches wide across the stripes.

Using small scissors, cut scallops from each stripe, leaving a quarter inch at the base. These will be the petals of your flower. The scalloped ribbon, wound in a circle, gives a sense of the final flower.

A petaled base is cut from the red wool. If you like, you can use a fabric marker to draw a circle and create a guideline for the petals to be sewn on.

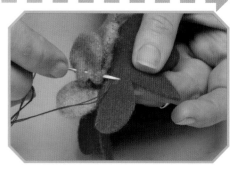

After securing your thread to the base, feed it through the bottom of the first petal twice as shown to create a pleated effect.

Insert the thread back through the base about 1/3 of the distance of the actual petal width and pull tightly to create a scalloped look.

Continue to string a round of petals in the same way, following your guideline on the base.

The second round of petals will begin just a quarter inch in from the first. After knotting off the thread holding the first round, I begin the second from the back.

After the second round of petals is sewn on, a final knot is set in the back to secure the petals.

Blanket stitching with a contrasting, doubled yarn creates a pretty finish for the petals. The flower is apt to want to curl and twist with all this sewing. Don't worry. After everything is sewn, push, pull, and stretch it into a pleasing shape. Felt can take it.

Cut out a circle big enough to comfortably cover the stitches on the back of the flower.

Sew your pin back on to the circle, secure it to the flower with pins, and then blanket stitch the backing on.

The finished back.

Individual Petals

By cutting out each petal individually, you can add texture and depth to your flower, sculpting flowers with even more three-dimensional appeal. Attaching each piece allows you to puff, curl, and pleat to create curled petals for beautiful effect.

This red rose was crafted using slightly larger petals in back from a thicker, somewhat darker felt than the slightly smaller petals in front, cut from a thinner wool scrap.

I love this plaid sunflower, it's perfect with jeans, or a jean jacket. The technique isn't limited to plaid, though, and is applicable to all kinds and shapes of flower petals. Plaid is a nice pattern to start with, though – its geometric nature makes it easier to cut like-sized petals.

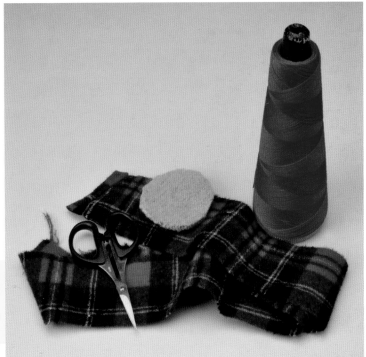

I am using a base circle cut from a wonderful thick golden sweater. A man's plaid shirt rips nicely into two-inch strips, and a matching embroidery thread will suffice for the entire project.

I don't want all my petals to be exactly alike, just roughly the same. I use my thumb as a rough template to gauge the width of each petal, and the strip determines the length.

Cut out a bunch. The bases of the petals don't need to be perfect – they won't show.

Fold the base of a petal into thirds, overlapping the two corners of the bottom, then secure it to the base. Because this flower has relatively long petals, work well in from the outer edge of the base to help provide support for the petals.

Leave a half-petal space between the first row of petals so you can get a nice, staggered second row, set tightly in between and just slightly further in than the first row.

After all the petals are secured, you'll need to cover the inner ends with something. Coiled fabric, a cutout circle, or thick blanket-stitching can accomplish this. Create a centerpiece from the old inseam of the sweater, removing and trimming this nice thick chunk of felt.

Measure the felted center, shaping it to overlap the ends of the petals, and then cutting at an angle so the ends overlap.

Two finished backs. Backs clearly don't have to be pretty, but a nicely finished back elevates your work to a higher artistic level.

Start whip stitching the center at the staggered end and continue around.

The overlap, where the two ends of the center come together, is shown in the foreground of this flower. It's only noticeable if you're looking for it.

To create a back, cut a circle big enough to overlap the central circle by at least a quarter inch on all sides. Pick a complementary thread.

Pin back to flower and whipstitch the backing, making it curl around the flower base. Halfway done, I remembered the pin back. I had enough room to attach it before closing the circle.

Finish stitching and tie off thread under the overlap of the circles.

Pull loose ends through the center and trim flush with the fabric.

Attaching a Leaf Back

A nice green leaf makes a natural foil for any pretty flower, and is an easy way to finish off the backs of your floral creations. Templates are provided for single and double leaf backs for your creations, but you'll probably need to make adjustments to suit your unique flowers. Recycled felt is cheap and blanket stitches are easy to pull out and redo — don't be afraid to make mistakes.

Cut two mirror image leaf backs in a size appropriate to your flower, overlapping the stitches in the back circle just a little bit.

After attaching the pinback to the outer leaf, pin the front and back pieces of the leaf to the flower and begin to blanket stitch the rounded edge of the leaf where it meets the flower back.

Continue to blanket stitch around the edge that meets the flower back.

You need to add a small knot to the point of the leaf to ensure that it doesn't slip free of the stitches.

After blanket stitching around the outer edge of the leaf, whip stitch the underside of the leaf to the remaining side of the flower. Make sure your stitches don't go all the way through and show on the outer leaf.

A little green leaf protrudes from behind a plaid sunflower.

To Dye For

To vary the routine, try creating a two dimensional flower while adding a little zest of your own – custom dying your felt. There's no need for bubbling cauldrons and caustic chemicals for this quick and fragrant process. The secret is Kool-Aid®, the pure powder sans sugar. The three pansies shown were created using Grape and Orange flavors, but there is a rainbow of other colors you can sample. This is a fun project, and each piece is guaranteed to be unique. In addition to French knots for the centers, try experimenting with beads, or metallic floss for a real eye-popping effect.

What you'll need: Black string and black felt. Light colored felt. Kool-Aid® in your choice of colors, and two tones of embroidery floss of like color. You'll also need a paintbrush, small scissors, pins, and needle. Use plastic wrap or something waterproof to protect your work surface. You might also want to wear gloves.

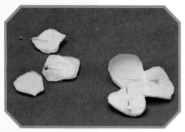

Trace and cut out the six pieces in Pattern Template 3 for the pansy, and two larger than anticipated circles to create the background, leaving room to trim later.

Soak the pansy pieces you plan to dye in water first so they will be wet. Put about a teaspoon of water on a saucer and add a minute amount of Kool-Aid® powder to the dish.

Paint on your center pattern. Be creative. Look at seed catalogs (there are lots of them online) and study different pansies. The variations are endless. The Grape flavor will fade to purples and blues as it dries overnight. Set the color using an iron, placing the dyed piece between two rags.

Attach the three smaller pieces on three sides, using two strands of the lighter color floss. The center will be covered and does not need to be secured.

Position the larger top piece and secure with pins. Again, let yourself be creative as you embellish the dyed areas with sprays of the darker colored floss. That blue spot on my hand is actually there – a casualty of using Kool-Aid® without gloves. The discoloration lasts for up to two days.

Now blanket stitch around the petals. Remember, the first stitch is a knot to secure the loop.

Add French knots or small beads in a random pattern to the center as embellishments. Let your muse be your guide.

When you're satisfied with your embroidery, pin the flower to a second layer of black felt and cut around your creation, leaving about an eighth of an inch reveal. If you are going to sew on a pin back, do so at this time to the outside of the backing.

Using a black thread, blanket stitch the two black layers together. Push your stitches right up against the stitches that secure the petals to make your flower even more secure.

Now Go Play

Following are some basic forms you can use for leaf backs, for flower backs, and for finishing flowers to cap your loopy creations. Pair a few wool scraps you like, grab a yarn that's friendly to work with, and start stitching things together. Have fun.

Four tiers make this flower seem complex, but it was pretty simple. A patterned sweater was used to create the alternate rows of loops, and two solid pieces of felt form the flower base and the third tier.

Two rows of thick, angora loops crown the basic flower base.

A button forms a solid center for a three-tiered flower formed from loops of striped sweater felt.

The double leaf base forms a nice foil for two flowers crafted from earthy tones.

Have you created some particularly pretty flowers? Give yourself an award. The same principles used to create a flower were used to craft this prize. Instead of leaves, a ribbon was cut from a striped sweater and used as a back. Pin one on; you deserve it!

The flower base has been blanket stitched to create a colorful background, capped by the thick, scored ribs of a sweater and a soft central piece.

An inner seam from a particularly fluff sweater makes a nice center.

Making a Hat

This hat is so easy you'll want to own one in every possible match for your favorite coats. It's quickly accessorized with different flower or heart brooches, too. To get started, you'll need a felt fabric to form the base of the hat, and a complementary felt for a decorative brim. Hand sewing is possible, but a sewing machine turns this project into a quick and easy, one-night project. If you like, hand-embellish with some blanket-stitching later.

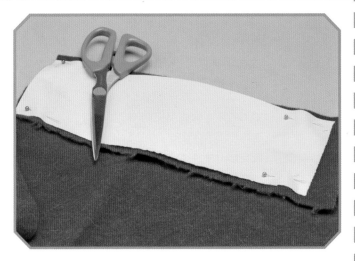

Measure your head at its widest point with a tape measure and add an inch for seams. In my case, I started with a 22-inch head measurement, and added an inch for 23 inches. Dividing that in half, I created a template 11 1/2 inches long by 4 1/2 inches deep. Because my felt is not 23 inches long, I cut two pieces with this template for the rim of the hat.

Luckily, our shrunken sweater is just right as is – we can cut out the 4 1/2-inch brim from the waistline.

A standard salad plate makes a great template for the crown. This one measures just over 7 1/2 inches in diameter. Experiment to find a circle that works best for your head shape. Using a grease pencil or fabric marker, trace around the edge and cut out.

Ready for sewing.

Line up the best sides of the hat brim facing each other. In other words, make sure matching sides of the felt are facing each other. Then seam the two together, creating a band. Iron seams open. Fold the crown both ways, mark four equidistant points around the perimeter.

Turn the hat right side out and shape it. Stretch and smush freely – felt is tough stuff. Fold the brim under and pin into shape.

Iron open the rim seams.

Pin the rim and the crown together, at first by quarters, and then again in halves. The rim is still inside out, with the seams on the outside. Make sure that if your felt is two-sided, you have matched top to sides.

Sew crown and rim together with a small, 1/4-inch seam.

A form is certainly helpful as you shape the hat, but not necessary. A volunteer, or a mirror, are other ways of making sure you're happy with the way the hat is shaping up.

Turn the hat right side out and pin brim to rim, right to wrong side. Again, work from quarters and then line up halfway points in between with pins.

Sew brim to rim.

When you're satisfied with the size and shape of the brim, baste it into shape with a whipstitch. I prefer to hide the stitches, but decorative stitching is certainly another option.

Hats are a wonderful way to express yourself. When they're made out of wool, they are genuinely warm, too.

A checked sweater gets a new life, forming a fat brim for a stylish woolen cap.

Sweater Bag

This fun bag uses the three garments we took apart, along with a contrasting white yarn that adds a little sparkle to the finished mix. A great big fluffy sweater that's been felted is the basis of the bag. The lining of a red jacket is used to create a lining for the purse. This isn't necessary, but it does make the bag that much nicer. In addition to the wool and selected yarn, you'll need about 5 1/2 feet of cotton clothesline for the handle.

Pattern Template 4

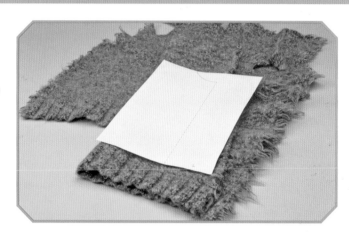

Starting with a piece of standard, 8 1/2-inch paper, I created a half template for the purse 5 1/2 inches wide to create a piece of wool 11 inches wide by 11 inches tall. I'll need two pieces of wool big enough to fold and cut out this shape. The semicircle was created using an old CD as a template. It is smaller than the final neck

Pin the template to the first piece of wool and cut out. I thought it would be fun to include the waistline ribbing from the sweater as the base of the purse.

Instead of using the paper pattern again, line up the front of the purse with a piece for the back, pin them, and cut.

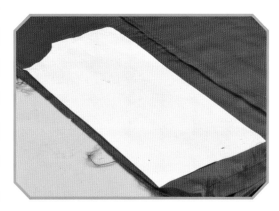

Using the same paper template, cut two pieces of the satin jacket lining just like the purse. These pieces, because of the tailored nature of the lining, will have a central seam running through them. Align the template to allow for the seam in the center. Err on the side of cutting too big – the lining should be the same or slightly bigger than the purse it will fill.

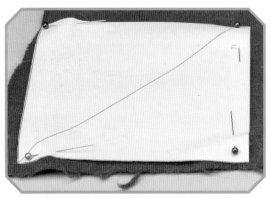

Cut four pieces of clothesline 16 inches long each and create four two-inch strips of wool to finish each.

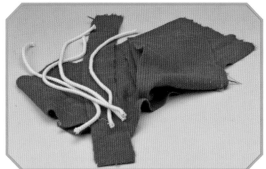

Remember, you can rip wool very nicely. After testing for the direction of the fabric grain, start your two-inch cut with scissors and pull.

Created a paper template 5 1/2 inches square and draw a line cross corner.

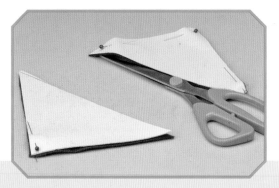

The triangles are cut out. These pieces will form anchors for the handles.

Pick a design to embellish your purse – a flower, a squirrel, a horse, or whatever you like. Here the same flower pattern we used as a base in creating brooches is traced onto freezer paper and ironed to the wool that matches the handles.

After cutting out the pattern, the freezer paper can be gently peeled away and reused time and again.

A small heart gives the flower the happy look I'm after. Select yarn that will contrast and show off the two elements.

After blanket stitching the heart to the flower, choose the best placement for the embellishment on the front piece of the purse (in this case off-center), pin it in place, and stitch.

Place the good sides, or the outsides, of the purse in, pin together, and sew the front and back together. You only need a small seam allowance, since this is thick wool and will be bulky. Moreover, since it's felt, you don't need to concern yourself with fraying!

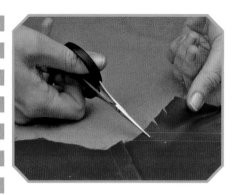

To prepare the lining, create small radial cuts around the curved neckline of the purse.

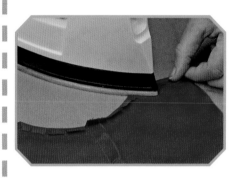

Press a quarter inch hem toward the inside of the lining.

Secure the hem.

Pin and sew the front and back lining together, good sides in.

Pin the bottom of bag and lining together and quickly whip stitch them together to hold the lining in place when the bag is turned right-side out.

After turning the bag right side out, baste stitch the top of the lining to the bag, about an inch from the brim. Be careful to keep your stitches from showing through on the front of the sweater bag.

Iron the bag into a shape that pleases you.

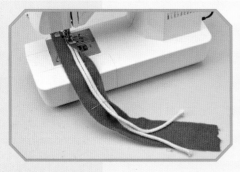

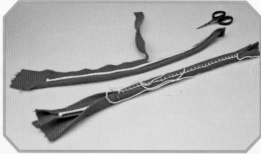

Stitch using a wide zigzag to connect wool and two ropes together.

Rip away excess wool and then add a second layer of two-inch wide wool with a contrasting blanket stitch.

The tops of the triangles can be cut off or folded under. Select a strong matching thread to connect the handle components.

Fold the trimmed triangle and sew, then turn right side out and fit over the handles.

Using a strong thread, attach the handles to the top of the bag. Stay close to the top of the sweater so the triangle can cover the stitches later.

Trim excess from the inner curve to make it fit tight against the handle.

The top of the bag is anchored all the way around the handles.

Accent yarn is tied to the handle...

... and the handle top is blanket stitched to the bag. The tail of the yarn is fed up through the wool and clipped flush to hide it.

Another finished sweater bag, this one was done with a wooly Irish sweater and men's suit fabric, nice earthy tones for the horse theme.

Patterns & Templates

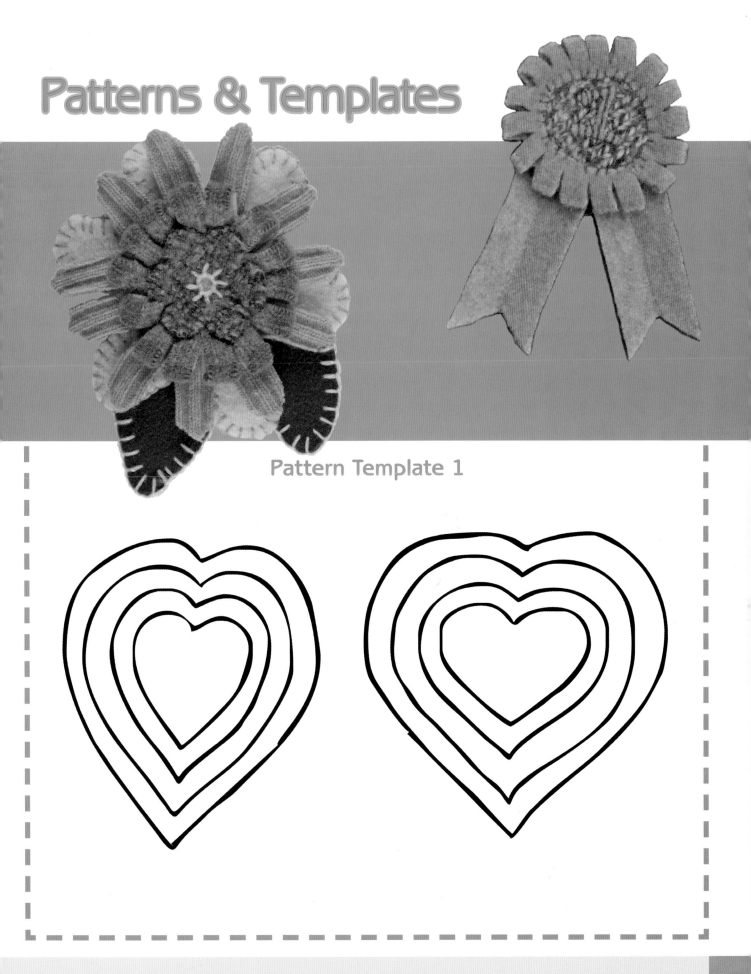

Pattern Template 1